PHOTO BY MARK AVERY

Ritch Brinkley, Daniel Mooney and Michael Tezla in a scene from the Milwaukee Repertory Theater production of "Villainous Company." Set and puppets designed by Laura Maurer.

VILLAINOUS COMPANY

A PLAY FOR THREE ACTORS

ADAPTED FROM *HENRY IV* AND

OTHER PLAYS OF SHAKESPEARE

BY AMLIN GRAY

**DRAMATISTS
PLAY SERVICE
INC.**

ADAPTOR'S NOTE

The Milwaukee Repertory Theater commissioned me to prepare a piece, easy to tour and based on Shakespeare, for their twenty-fifth season. This play is the result.

Villainous Company tells the story of Hal, the young hellion who is to become Henry V, and his long-delayed choice between the values of his father, Henry IV, and those of his surrogate father, Jack Falstaff. Most of its material is drawn, of course, from *Henry IV, Parts One and Two*. In an attempt to approximate Shakespeare's diction (and to ease the conscience of the adaptor), the necessary additional material has been drawn, wherever possible, from language, images, and conceits in various of Shakespeare's other plays. Devotees of the Bard will recognize lines and phrases from *All's Well That Ends Well, Henry V, Antony and Cleopatra, Hamlet, The Tempest, King John, Othello, King Lear, Twelfth Night, Macbeth, Romeo and Juliet,* and *Richard III.* But the spine of the play is the central action of *Henry IV, Part One.*

The particular concerns of the adaptation have been to make the plot clear — especially Hal's alternatives — and to emphasize that Falstaff, that feast of all the world's delights, the quickest and most hilariously deflationary mind in all the plays, is also an armed robber, an official who squeezes bribes from poor draftees, and a captain who leads his soldiers to their death so he can keep their pay.

I'm grateful to the Milwaukee Repertory Theater for asking me to put this piece together. And I'm grateful to the glover's son from Stratford. To meddle with his work, however clear the need and purpose, is the acme both of *hubris* and frustration. But it's shown me once again the breadth, the generosity, the *freedom* of Shakespeare's genius. He took everything life offers and he gave it back for all of us to have, forever.

A. G.

VILLAINOUS COMPANY was first performed by the Milwaukee Repertory Theater, John Dillon, Artistic Director, Sara O'Connor, Managing Director, on October 10, 1978. It was directed by John Dillon and Susan Einhorn. The set and the puppets were designed by Laura Maurer. The costumes were designed by Colleen Muscha. The fights were choreographed by Michael Tezla. The Stage Manager was Jay Moran. The cast was as follows:

ACTOR 1 . . . . Ritch Brinkley
ACTOR 2 . . . . Michael Tezla
ACTOR 3 . . . . Daniel Mooney

CAST OF CHARACTERS

Three actors play all of the play's eighteen roles, as follows:

> Actor 1   CHORUS
>   KING'S ATTENDANT
>   FALSTAFF
>   GILLIAMS (Voice off)
>   TAPSTER (Voice off)
>
> Actor 2   CHORUS
>   HENRY IV
>   BARDOLPH
>   HOTSPUR
>
> Actor 3   WESTMORELAND
>   CHORUS
>   HAL
>   MOLDY
>   SHADOW
>   WART
>   FEEBLE
>   BULLCALF
>   REBEL SOLDIER

SETTING

The play requires a backdrop with several breaks in it through which the actors can enter and exit. An onstage trunk might contain the mugs and the cushion used in the tavern scenes; it may also serve as a throne, a bench, etc., before being struck for the battle sequence. Backstage, a ladder or a table can help Bardolph make his first appearance at Gad's Hill over the top of the backdrop.

"Company, villainous company,
hath been the spoil of me."

— *Henry IV, Part One,*
Act III, Scene 3

VILLAINOUS COMPANY

(Drum roll. Actors 1 and 2 enter around opposite sides of the backdrop. Actor 1 carries a robe and crown.)

CHORUS—Actor 1. The nineteenth year of the embattled reign
Of sovereign Henry, fourth king of that name,
A rebel lord gan raise a mighty power
Whose aim was no less than King Henry's crown.
CHORUS—Actor 2. But here we'll pause, if you will give us leave,
While I, the actor who will play the king,
First play the beggar: we must ask your help.
Can this bare platform represent a palace?
May we cram within these few square yards
The bloody field where Henry met his foes?
We can: with your best fancies to assist us.
CHORUS—Actor 1. Think, when we talk of horses, that you see them
Printing their proud hoofs in the receiving earth;
For 'tis your thoughts that now must deck our kings.
CHORUS—Actor 2. As we begin, imagine this the room
All hung with gold where Henry keeps his state.
A perfumed censer strokes the sense with fragrance.
(Taking the crown from Actor 1.)
Now come with us. Let your minds take wing.
An actor speaks, but you must hear the king.
(With the last words, he has solemnly lowered the crown onto his head and Actor 1 has invested him in the royal robe. Now Actor 1 kneels in obeisance.)
HENRY—Actor 2. Is Lord Westmoreland in attendance here?
ATTENDANT—Actor 1. He is, my lord, and waits to know your pleasure.
HENRY. Bid him come before us. *(The Attendant hurries off. King Henry, deeply troubled, walks a pace or two downstage. Enter Westmoreland—Actor 3. He kneels.)*

WESTMORELAND.   I commend
My love and duty to your Majesty.
HENRY. I thank you, cousin Westmoreland. What news
Now from our men who watch the restless North?
WESTMORELAND. They say the army whereof rumor
speaks
Still gathers head, that now their numbers threaten.
HENRY. Who doth lead them? Have they found out that?
WESTMORELAND. The eldest son of old Northumberland,
The gallant Harry Hotspur, is their chief,
Whose reputation with a sword is such
'Twould be a sight indeed if one could match him.
HENRY. Yea, there thou mak'st me sad, and mak'st me sin
In envy that my Lord Northumberland
Should be the father to so brave a son,
A son who is the theme of honor's tongue,
Whilst I, by looking on the praise of him,
See riot and dishonor stain the brow
Of my young Harry. O that it could be proved
That some night-tripping fairy had exchanged
In cradle-clothes our children where they lay.
Then would I have his Harry, and he mine.
But can you tell me where my son is now?
I have not seen him in a month and more.
WESTMORELAND. My liege, I know not.
HENRY.   Let him from my thoughts.
I'll walk a turn or two about the garden.
When there's further tidings, seek me there.
WESTMORELAND. I will, my liege. God send your Grace
fair thoughts. (*King Henry exits. Turning downstage, Actor 3 removes
a costume item — probably a hat — and speaks to the audience as Chorus.*)
CHORUS. Most subject is the richest soil to weeds;
The king's son, Hal, seems overspread with them.
While foemen of his father gather strength,
Hal spends his nights and sleeps away his days
In Eastcheap, in a tavern with his friends.
(*During the next lines, Bardolph — Actor 2, wearing a red false
nose — and Falstaff — Actor 1 — come in and lie down "passed out" on the
floor. Bardolph leans against Falstaff's enormous girth.*)
This man, one Bardolph, has a nose as red

10

As wine, which nightly tucks him into bed.
And Sir John Falstaff, who was born a knight,
Fell victim to hard times — without a fight.
(*He exits. Falstaff snorts and rolls over. Bardolph stirs, stands up, prodigiously hung over, totally disoriented. As He begins to realize where he is, nausea strikes. He claps his hand over his mouth and runs off. Hal — Actor 3 — comes in, also the worse for the night gone by. He teases Falstaff awake by squirting wine in his face from a wineskin. Falstaff wakes up, stretches luxuriously, but stays lying or sitting, enjoying his repose.*)

FALSTAFF. Now, Hal, what time of day is it, lad?

HAL. Thou art so fat-witted from drinking of dry sack, and unbuttoning thee after supper, and sleeping upon benches after noon, that thou hast forgotten to demand that truly which thou would'st truly know. What the devil hast thou to do with the time of the day? Unless hours were cups of sack, and minutes chickens roasting on a spit, unless clocks were the tongues of bawds, and sundials were the signs of leaping houses — I see no reason why thou should'st be so superfluous as to demand the time of the day.

FALSTAFF. Indeed, you come near me now, Hal. (*He matter-of-factly takes Hal's wineskin and pours a sizable drink — medicinal, for his hangover — into a mug he finds overturned on the floor. This done, he will take illustrative drinks during his speech.*) A good sherry-sack hath a twofold operation in it. It ascends me into the brain; dries me there all the foolish and dull and curdled vapors which environ it, makes it apprehensive, quick, full of nimble, fiery and delectable shapes. The second property of your excellent sherris is the warming of the blood, which before, cold and settled, left the liver white and pale, which is the very badge of cowardice. But the sherris warms it, and makes it course from the innards to the parts extreme. It illumineth the face, which, as a beacon, gives warning to all the rest of this little kingdom, man, to arm! and this valor comes of sherris. And this is the reason that thou art valiant. For the cold blood thou didst naturally inherit of thy father, thou hast, like lean, sterile and bare land, manured and tilled with excellent endeavor of drinking good, and good store of, fertile sherris, that thou art become very hot and valiant. If I had a thousand sons, the first humane principle I would teach them should be to forswear thin potations and to addict themselves to sack. (*He drinks off the rest of the*

11

mug.) I prithee, sweet wag, shall there be gallows standing in England when thou art king? And good lusty fellows like me put down by lawmakers? Do not, when thou art king, hang a thief.

HAL. No. Thou shalt.

FALSTAFF. Shall I? O rare! By the Lord, I'll be a splendid judge!

HAL. Thou judgest false already. I mean that thou shalt hang the thieves, and so become a splendid hangman.

FALSTAFF. Enough, and too much, of this foolishness. Thou hast done much harm upon me, Hal—God forgive thee for it! Before I knew thee I knew nothing; and now am I, if a man should speak truly, little better than one of the wicked. I must give over this life, and I will give it over! I'll be damned for no king's son in Christendom.

HAL. Where shall we steal a purse tomorrow, Jack?

FALSTAFF. Zounds, where thou wilt, lad! I'll be there! If I be not, hang me upside down.

HAL. I see a good reform of life in thee: from praying to purse-taking.

FALSTAFF. Why, Hal, 'tis my vocation, Hal; 'tis no sin for a man to labor in his vocation. (*Re-enter Bardolph.*)

HAL. Here comes Bardolph.

FALSTAFF. O, if men were to be saved by merit, what hole in hell were hot enough for him? I never see thy face but I think upon hell-fire, for there the damned are in that nose of thine, burning, burning!

BARDOLPH. Why, Sir John, my nose does you no harm.

FALSTAFF. (*Gesturing with Hal's wineskin.*) I have maintained that salamander of yours with fire for two-and-thirty years, may God reward me for it!

BARDOLPH. 'Sblood, I would my nose were in your belly.

FALSTAFF. God have mercy! so should I be sure to be heart-burnt.

HAL. Bardolph, what's the news?

BARDOLPH. Tomorrow morning, by four o'clock early at Gad's Hill, there are tax-collectors riding to London with the King's own purse in keeping. We may rob them as secure as sleep.

FALSTAFF. Hal, wilt thou make one?

HAL. Not I, by my faith.

12

FALSTAFF. By the Lord, I'll be a traitor, then, when thou art king.

HAL. I care not.

BARDOLPH. Come with us, my lord.

FALSTAFF. There's neither honesty, manhood, nor good fellowship in thee, nor thou camest not of the blood royal, if thou darest not — just for recreation's sake — forget true prince to play false thief.

HAL. Well, then, once in my life I'll be a madcap.

FALSTAFF. Why that's well said. Bardolph, come along with me. Farewell, sweet wag. Till four o'clock — at Gad's Hill!

HAL. Farewell, my sweet creature of bombast. (*To the audience.*) I will make a jest of this exploit, and a week of laughter of these highwaymen. They look for me at four o'clock. I'll be there, but behind a tree. They'll set on the carriers by themselves, and when they have the booty I'll disguise myself and rob the thieves. It won't be hard to face them from their prize. This Bardolph is as true-bred coward as ever turned back. For Barebone Jack, if he fight longer than he sees reason then I'll eat my sword. The cream of the jest will be the unimaginable lies that this same fat rogue will tell; how thirty at least he fought with; what thrusts, what blows, what extremities he endured; and in the puncturing this bladder lies the jest. I am not yet of Harry Hotspur's mind, the hero of the North; he that kills some six or seven dozen enemies before breakfast, washes his hands and says to his wife, "Fie upon this quiet life, I want work!" And so I play the fool with the time, though the spirits of the wise sit in the clouds and mock me. Tomorrow morning, four o'clock, at Gad's Hill! (*He exits. Hotspur — Actor 2 — strides on. He carries riding boots, the spurs of which he polishes.*)

HOTSPUR. What ho! Where's Gilliams? Harry Hotspur calls!

GILLIAMS — Actor 1. (*Behind the drop.*) I'm here, my lord.

HOTSPUR. Hath Butler brought my horse?

GILLIAMS. One horse, my lord, he's bringing even now.

HOTSPUR. What horse? A roan, a crop-ear, is it not?

GILLIAMS. It is, my lord.

HOTSPUR.   That roan shall be my throne.
Well, I will back him straight. O Esperance!
Tomorrow we set forth. And Hal, the madcap,
Best had look unto his father's crown.
By heaven, methinks it were an easy leap

13

To pluck bright honor from the pale-faced moon
Or dive into the bottom of the deep,
Where fathom-line could never touch the ground,
And pluck up drownèd honor by the hair!
(*A whinny is heard from behind the drop.*)
My horse is come! O let the hours be short
Till fields and blows and groans applaud our sport!
(*He exits around the drop. Gad's Hill. Hal comes on, carrying a lantern, and looks around.*)
FALSTAFF. (*Off.*) Bardolph? (*Whistles a signal; or tries to but is too short of breath.*) Bardolph! (*Hal runs behind the drop and hides. Falstaff enters, carrying a lantern. To audience, panting and puffing.*) Bardolph is gone to the top of the hill to look out for the carriers, and now cannot I find him. If I travel but four foot further afoot, I shall break my wind. (*Tries to whistle again.*) Bardolph! (*To audience again.*) And the true prince played us false as water. A king's son! Ha! If I do not beat him out of his kingdom with a toothpick, and drive all his subjects before me like a flock of wild geese, I would I might never wear hair on my face more. (*A noise off. Falstaff flattens—as flat as he goes.*)
BARDOLPH. (*Appears over the drop, or around it.*) Sst! Who's there? Is that you, Sir John?
FALSTAFF. That nose of thine is better than a lantern.
BARDOLPH. Draw thy sword. There's money of the King's coming down the hill. Tis going to the King's treasury.
FALSTAFF. You lie, you rogue. 'Tis going to the Prince's tavern. How many be there of them?
BARDOLPH. Some three or four.
FALSTAFF. Zounds, will they not rob us?
BARDOLPH. Stand to. They're coming. (*He disappears.*)
FALSTAFF. (*Runs off, shouting.*) Strike! Down with them! Cut the villains' throats! These parasites and bacon-eaters hate us youth! Down with them! Fleece them! Carbonado their shanks!
CARRIERS—Actors 2 and 3. (*From offstage.*) O we are undone! Have mercy! O! (*Hal comes on as if to get a better view.*)
HAL. (*To the audience.*) The thieves have bound the true men. Now could I rob the thieves and go merrily to London, it were laughter for a month and a good jest forever. (*He hides behind the drop again as Falstaff and Bardolph come on with bags of money.*)
FALSTAFF. Well done, Bardolph. Let us share, and then to horse before day. If the Prince be not an arrant coward, there's

14

no equity stirring. The boy has no more valor than a rabbit. (*Slipping on a mask, Hal rushes upon them waving his sword and making a terrific racket.*)

HAL. Your money, villains! Die the death! What? I am for thee, rascals! Stand and fight! (*Bardolph flees without a second's thought. Falstaff fights a blow or two, then, seeing himself bettered, follows Bardolph. They leave their booty behind.*) Got with much ease. Now merrily to horse. Falstaff sweats to death and lards the lean earth as he walks along. Were't not for laughing, I should pity him. How the rogue roared! (*He exits with the moneybags. Henry IV alone in his throne room.*)

HENRY. How many thousand of my poorest subjects
Are at this hour asleep? O sleep, O gentle sleep,
Nature's soft nurse, how have I frighted thee
That thou no more wilt weigh mine eyelids down
And steep my senses in forgetfulness?
The peasant, happy in his state, lies down.
Uneasy lies the head that wears a crown.
(*Enter Westmoreland.*) Thy looks are full of speed. What is thy news?

WESTMORELAND. Young Hotspur and his rebel forces meet
The eleventh of this month at Shrewsbury.
A mighty and a fearful head they are
As ever offered foul play in a state.

HENRY. But where is my son Harry all this while?
Nay, tell me not. I know it all too well.
The Prince debauches with his tavern-friends
While treason's clamor shakes our very throne.
He's like enough, through base and slavish fear,
To fight against me under Hotspur's pay,
To dog his heels and curtsy at his frowns
To show how much he is degenerate.

WESTMORELAND. Do not say so. You will not find it so.
The Prince but studies his companions
Like a strange tongue, whereof to learn the language
'Tis needful that the most immodest word
Be studied with the rest; which once attained,
Your Highness knows, comes to no further use
But to be known and hated. So, like gross words,
The Prince will, in the perfectness of time,

15

Cast off his followers, and their memory
Shall as a pattern or a measure live
By which his Grace may judge the lives of others,
Turning past evils to advantages.

HENRY. It may be so.

WESTMORELAND. I swear it is no other.

HENRY. Send for the Prince. Make haste. 'Tis almost day.
Advantage feeds him fat while men delay.

(*They exit in opposite directions. The tavern. Hal is heard, idly singing. After a moment, he strolls in.*)

HAL. When that I was and a little tiny boy
With hey ho the wind and the rain
A foolish life was all my joy
For the rain it raineth every day.

TAPSTER—Actor 1. (*Voice off.*) My lord, Sir John and Bardolph are at the door. Shall I let them in?

HAL. Let them alone a while, and then open the door.

TAPSTER. I will, my lord.

HAL. (*Sings.*) But when I came to man's estate
With hey ho the wind and the rain
'Gainst fools and thieves men shut their gate
For the rain it raineth every day.

(*Enter Falstaff and Bardolph: both with mugs and Bardolph with a cask of wine.*)

HAL. Welcome, Jack. Where hast thou been?

FALSTAFF. A plague of all cowards, I say, and a vengeance too! marry and amen! Fill me a cup of sack, Bardolph! A plague of all cowards! Is there no virtue extant?

HAL. How now, blown Jack, what mutter you?

FALSTAFF. The rogues! Here's water in this sack, too! There is nothing but roguery to be found in villainous man. Yet a coward is worse than a cup of sack with water in it. Go thy ways, old Jack, die when thou wilt; if manhood, good manhood, be not forgot upon the face of the earth, then I pray God my girdle break.

HAL. And if it did, how would thy guts fall about thy knees.

FALSTAFF. There live not three good men unhanged in England, and one of them is fat and grows old. A plague of all cowards, I say still.

HAL. Why, you whoreson round man, what's the matter?

FALSTAFF. Are you not a coward? Answer me to that! (*To*

16

Bardolph.) Give me a cup of sack! I am a rogue if I have drunk today.

HAL. O villain! Thy lips are scarce wiped since thou drunkest last.

FALSTAFF. All's one for that. A plague of all cowards, still say I.

HAL. What's the matter?

FALSTAFF. What's the matter? There be two of us here have ta'en a thousand pounds this morning.

HAL. Where is it, Jack? Where is it?

FALSTAFF. Where is it? Taken from us it is. A hundred upon poor two of us.

HAL. What, a hundred, man?

FALSTAFF. I am a rogue if I were not hand-to-hand with a dozen of them. I have 'scaped by miracle. I am eight times thrust through the doublet, four through the hose. My sword was hacked like a handsaw, ecce signum! (*He shows his sword.*) I never fought better since I was a man. All would not do. A plague of all cowards! Let Bardolph speak. If he speaks more or less than truth, he is a villain and the son of darkness.

HAL. (*To Bardolph.*) Speak. How was it?

BARDOLPH. We two set upon some four—

FALSTAFF. Sixteen at least, my lord.

BARDOLPH. And bound them—no, they were not bound.

FALSTAFF. You rogue, they were bound, every man of them!

BARDOLPH. As we were sharing, some six or seven fresh men set upon us—

FALSTAFF. And unbound the rest, and then come in the other.

HAL. What, fought ye with them all?

FALSTAFF. All? I know not what ye call all, but if I fought not with fifty of them, I am a bunch of radish. If there were not two or three and fifty upon poor old Jack, then am I no two-legged creature.

HAL. Pray God you have not murdered some of them.

FALSTAFF. Nay, that's past praying for. I have peppered two of them. Two I am sure I paid. I tell thee what, Hal—if I tell thee a lie, spit in my face, call me horse. Thou knowest my old battle stance; here I stood, and thus I bore my point. Four rogues let drive at me—

HAL. What, four? Thou said'st but two even now.

17

FALSTAFF. Four, Hal, I told thee four. These four all thrust at me. I made no more ado but took all their seven points on my shield, thus.

HAL. Seven? Why, there were but four even now.

FALSTAFF. Seven, by this hilt, or I am a villain else. Thou dost not mark me.

HAL. Yes I do.

FALSTAFF. These nine rogues that I told thee of began to give me ground. But I followed close, came in foot and hand, and, quick as thought, seven of the eleven I paid!

HAL. O monstrous! Eleven men grown out of two!

FALSTAFF. But, as the devil would have it, three misbegotten knaves in Kendal green came at my back and let drive at me; for it was so dark, Hal, that thou could'st not see thy hand—

HAL. These lies are like the father that begets them—gross as a mountain, open, palpable. Why, thou clay-brained guts, thou paunch, thou midriff, thou whoreson obscene greasy tallow-catch—

FALSTAFF. What, art thou mad! Is not the truth the truth?

HAL. How could'st thou know these men in Kendal green when it was so dark thou could'st not see thy hand? Come, tell me your reason. What sayest thou to this?

FALSTAFF. What, upon command? If I were under torture, I'd not tell you on command. Give you a reason on command! If reasons were as plentiful as raisins I would give no man a reason on command, not I.

HAL. I'll be no longer guilty of this sin; this red-faced coward, this bed-presser, this horse-back-breaker, this huge hill of flesh—

FALSTAFF. 'Sblood, you starveling, you elf-skin, you dried ox-tongue, you bull's pizzle—O for breath to utter what is like thee—you tailor's yardstick, you sheath, you bowcase, you rapier with feet!—

HAL. Well, catch your breath and then to it again. But first just hear me speak one word. And mark me, Jack. I saw you two set on four and make yourselves the masters of their wealth. Mark you now how a plain tale shall put you down. Then did I set on you two by myself and chase you from your prize, which I can show you right here in the house. And, Falstaff, you carried your guts away as nimbly, and roared for mercy, and still ran and roared, as ever I heard bull-calf. What a slave art thou to hack thy sword as thou hast done and then say it was in fight! What trick, what hiding place, canst thou now find out to shield thee from this open and apparent shame?

FALSTAFF. By the Lord, I knew ye as well as he that made ye. Why, hear you, my lord. Was it for me to kill the heir-apparent? Should I turn upon the true prince? Why, thou knowest I am as valiant as Hercules, but beware instinct. The lion will not touch the true prince. Instinct is a great matter. I was now a coward on instinct. I shall think the better of myself and thee during my life — I for a valiant lion, and thou for a true prince. But by the Lord, lad, I am glad you have the money. What? Shall we be merry? Shall we make a play up on the spot?

HAL. Let's have a play about my father. Thou shalt play him.

FALSTAFF. Shall I? Be thou warned, ungracious puppy. I shall chide thee for an unfilial son.

HAL. I pray you do. I shall practice an answer.

FALSTAFF. And thou hast need. Thou'lt play this scene in earnest one day.

HAL. Do thou stand for my father and examine me on the particulars of my life.

FALSTAFF. Content. This bench shall be my throne, this sword my scepter, and this cushion my crown. Give me a cup of sack to make my eyes look red, that it may be thought that I have wept. (*Bardolph fills Falstaff's mug.*)

HAL. (*Kneeling.*) Well, here is my knee.

FALSTAFF. And here is my speech. Harry, I do not only marvel where thou spendest thy time, but also how thou art accompanied. Doth the blessed sun of heaven prove a truant and eat blackberries? A question not to be asked. Shall the son of England prove a thief and take purses? A question to be asked. There is a thing, Harry, which thou hast often heard of, and it is known to many in our land by the name of pitch. This pitch, as ancient writers do report, doth defile; so doth the company thou keepest. And yet — there is a virtuous man whom I have often noted in thy company, but I know not his name.

HAL. What manner of man, so please your Majesty?

FALSTAFF. A goodly portly man, i'faith, and a corpulent; of a cheerful look, a pleasing eye, and a most noble carriage; and, as I think, his age some fifty — (*Bardolph makes a "raspberry" sound.*) Or, by'r Lady, inclining to three-score; and now I remember, his name is Falstaff. If that man should be lewdly given he deceiveth me, for, Harry, I see virtue in his looks. If, then, the tree may be known by the fruit as the fruit by the tree, there is virtue in that Falstaff. Him keep with, the rest banish. And tell me now, thou naughty varlet, tell me, where hast thou been this month?

HAL. Dost thou speak like a king? Do thou stand for me, and I'll play my father.

FALSTAFF. Depose me? If thou dost it half so majestically, hang me up by the heels for a suckling rabbit.

HAL. Well, here I am set.

FALSTAFF. And here I stand. Judge you, Bardolph.

HAL. Now, Harry, whence come you?

FALSTAFF. My noble lord, from Eastcheap.

HAL. The complaints I hear of thee are grievous.

FALSTAFF. 'Sblood, my lord, they are false!

HAL. Thou art violently carried away from grace. There is a devil haunts thee in the likeness of an old fat man; a ton of man is thy companion. Why dost thou converse with that stuffed cloak-bag of guts, that roasted Manningtree ox with the pudding in his belly, that father ruffian, that gray iniquity? Wherein is he good, but to taste sack and drink it? Wherein neat and cleanly, but to carve a chicken and eat it? Wherein skillful, but in villainy? Wherein villainous, but in all things? Wherein worthy, but in nothing?

FALSTAFF. I would your Grace would take me with you. Whom means your Grace?

HAL. That villainous, abominable misleader of youth, Falstaff, that old white-bearded Satan.

FALSTAFF. My lord, the man I know.

HAL. I know thou dost.

FALSTAFF. But to say I know more harm in him than in myself were to say more than I know. That he is old his white hairs witness. But that he is, saving your Reverence, a whoremaster, that I utterly deny. If sack and sugar be a fault, God help the wicked. No, my lord. Banish Bardolph, banish all thy Harry's tavern full of friends. But for sweet Jack Falstaff, kind Jack Falstaff, true Jack Falstaff, valiant Jack Falstaff, banish not him thy Harry's company, banish not him thy Harry's company! Banish plump Jack, and banish all the world!

HAL. I do. I will. (*A knocking is heard.*) Bardolph, go see who's at the door.

FALSTAFF. Wait, my lord, play out the play. I have much to say on the behalf of that Falstaff.

BARDOLPH. (*Rushes in.*) My lord, it's Sir John Bracy, come from your father. An army of rebels is on the march. You must to the wars.

HAL. By Heaven, now I feel me much to blame
So idly to profane the precious time
While tempest of rebellion gathers clouds
And rains upon our bare unarmèd heads.
Falstaff, I commission you to raise
A company of soldiers. You'll have gold.
The land is burning. Hotspur stands on high.
And either he or I must lower lie.
(*He goes out.*)

FALSTAFF. (*To Bardolph.*) You see how men of merit are sought after? The undeserver may sleep, while the man of action is called on.

BARDOLPH. Well, farewell, Sir John. Have a care of thyself. I hope thou be not stabbed, or shot, or run through with a broadsword.

FALSTAFF. Farewell me no farewells, my lad. Thou art the King's man now. I draft thee.

BARDOLPH. But—

FALSTAFF. Come go with me. I'll show thee how I'll turn these wars to profit. Brave world! Corporal Bardolph, follow me! Left, right, left, right—(*He marches Bardolph out, as a drum is heard offstage. Actor 2 returns, not wearing the false nose, as Chorus.*)

CHORUS. Now all of England doth prepare for war.
Young Hotspur presses farmers from the fields
Belonging to the landlords in his barony.
King Henry bids his generals prepare
And gives each one of his civilian knights
A payroll of three hundred pounds in gold
To raise and pay a company of men.
Jack Falstaff is the first to draw his gold.
The first man Falstaff drafts, as you have seen,
Is one who'd sooner hear the devil roar
(*Putting on the red nose.*)
Than hear a drum; one Bardolph, namely—me.
(*Enter Falstaff. He has added some military appurtenance to his outfit—perhaps an armor breastplate or a helmet with a plume.*)

FALSTAFF. Well met, Corporal Bardolph.

BARDOLPH. (*Reluctantly.*) Good morrow, captain.

FALSTAFF. Have you procured me half a dozen men?

BARDOLPH. I have, Sir John— (*Correcting himself.*) Yes, captain.

FALSTAFF. Let me see them.

BARDOLPH. (*Searches his clothes as he crosses to the wings.*) Yes, sir, yes, sir, where's the roll? Come forward, sirs. (*Actor 3 enters with a rack of five rope- or broomstick-men with funny heads. These are Moldy, Shadow, Wart, Feeble, and Bullcalf. Actor 3 will do all their voices. Bardolph finds a sheet of paper.*) Ralph Moldy! Let you step forward as I call. Ralph Moldy!

MOLDY. (*"Stepping" forward.*) Here, an't please you.

BARDOLPH. (*To Falstaff..*) What think you, sir? A good-limbed fellow, young and strong.

FALSTAFF. Is thy name Moldy?

MOLDY. Yea, an't please you.

FALSTAFF. 'Tis the more time thou wert used. (*To Bardolph.*) Prick him.

BARDOLPH. (*Not understanding the word.*) Prick him?

FALSTAFF. Mark him down! (*Bardolph puts a mark by Moldy's name with a pencil.*)

MOLDY. My wife will be undone now for one to do her cooking and cleaning. You need not to have pricked me. There are other men fitter to go than I.

FALSTAFF. Go to, peace, Moldy, you shall go. Moldy, it is time you were spent.

MOLDY. Spent!

BARDOLPH. Peace, fellow, stand back. Know you where you are? (*Moldy gets back in line.*) Simon Shadow!

FALSTAFF. Yea, marry, let me have him to sit under.

BARDOLPH. Where's Shadow?

SHADOW. Here, sir.

FALSTAFF. Shadow will serve for summer. Prick him.

BARDOLPH. Thomas Wart!

FALSTAFF. Where's he?

WART. Here, sir.

FALSTAFF. Is thy name Wart?

WART. Yea, sir.

FALSTAFF. Thou art a very ragged wart.

BARDOLPH. Shall I prick him, Sir John?

FALSTAFF. It were superfluous, for he looks as he were pinned together. Prick him no more.

WART. O, thank you, sir! (*He "exits"—that is, he is tossed behind the drop by Actor 3.*)

BARDOLPH. Francis Feeble!

FEEBLE. Here, sir.

FALSTAFF. What trade art thou, Feeble?

FEEBLE. A woman's tailor, sir.

BARDOLPH. Shall I prick him, sir?

FALSTAFF. You may; but if he'd been a man's tailor he'd have pricked you. Wilt thou make as many holes in the enemy's lines as thou hast made in a woman's petticoat?

FEEBLE. I will do my best, sir. You can have no more.

FALSTAFF. Well said, courageous Feeble! Prick the woman's tailor!

FEEBLE. I would Wart might have gone, sir.

FALSTAFF. I would thou wert a man's tailor, that thou mightst mend him and make him fit to go. Who is next?

BARDOLPH. Peter Bullcalf of the Green.

FALSTAFF. Yea, marry, let us see Bullcalf.

BULLCALF. Here, sir.

FALSTAFF. 'Fore God, a likely fellow! Come, prick me Bullcalf till he roar.

BULLCALF. O Lord! Good my lord captain—

FALSTAFF. What, dost thou roar before thou art pricked?

BULLCALF. O Lord, sir, I am a diseased man.

FALSTAFF. What disease hast thou?

BULLCALF. A whoreson cold, sir, a cough, sir, that I caught at my brother's funeral.

FALSTAFF. Come, thou shalt go to the wars in a nightgown, and thy friends shall catch cold at thy funeral. Prick him! Good corporal, a word. (*Aside to Bardolph..*) Thou know'st what to do.

BARDOLPH. Ay.

FALSTAFF. (*To the Recruits.*) I'll be with you anon. Give the corporal the names of your next of kin. (*He exits. Bardolph pretends to write on his paper. Bullcalf edges towards him.*)

BULLCALF. Good Master Corporate Bardolph, stand my friend. I've twenty shillings for you. In very truth, sir, I'd as soon be hanged as go. And yet for mine own part, sir, I do not care, but rather because I am unwilling, and, for mine own part, have a desire to stay with my friends. Else, sir, I did not care for mine own part, so much.

BARDOLPH. Go to, stand aside. (*Bullcalf "exits."*)

MOLDY. And, good Master Corporal Captain, for my wife's sake, stand my friend. You shall have forty shillings, sir.

BARDOLPH. Go to, stand aside. (*"Exit" Moldy.*)

FEEBLE. By my troth, I care not. A man can die but once. No man's too good to serve his prince. And, let it go which way it will, he that dies this year owes nothing for the next.

BARDOLPH. Well said. Thou'rt a good fellow.

FEEBLE. Faith, I'll bear no base mind.

(*Re-enter Falstaff.*)

FALSTAFF. 'Tis time, sirs. We must march away. (*Aside to Bardolph.*) Our numbers dwindle. Doth our purse increase?

BARDOLPH. One pound for Bullcalf, two for Moldy.

FALSTAFF. God be thanked for these rebels. They offend none but the virtuous. Muster me another five at Mile End. (*Bardolph runs off.*) Gentlemen, we must a dozen mile tonight. Thou'rt soldiers now, so play the men! Straighten up there, Shadow! Advance, march! Left, right, left, right—(*He marches off his new recruits. Drum from offstage. The drum continues, or crossfades with a second drum, as Hotspur strides on and addresses his offstage troops.*)

HOTSPUR. Soldiers, friends, stand fast and give me ear.
Now Harry Hotspur speaks to you plain soldier.
The cause we undertake is dangerous—
But if we live, we live to tread on kings.
If die, brave death when princes die with us.
Let each man do his best. And here draw I
A sword whose temper I intend to stain
With the best blood that I can meet withal
In the adventure of this perilous day.
Now, Esperance! Hotspur, and set on!

(*Drum. Hotspur strides off. Hal comes on. He kneels as Henry IV enters from the opposite direction. Henry gestures to his offstage troops.*)

HENRY. Sirs, rest yourselves. The Prince of Wales and I
Must have some private conference alone.

(*To Hal.*)

I know not whether God will have it so
For some displeasing service I have done
That, in His judgment, out of my own blood

24

He'll breed revengement and a scourge for me.
But thou dost, in the wildness of thy life,
Make me believe that thou art only marked
For the hot vengeance and the rod of Heaven
To punish my mistreadings. How else could
Such barren pleasures, rude society,
As thou art matched withal and grafted to
Accompany the greatness of thy blood
And hold their level with thy princely heart?
HAL. So please your Majesty, I hope I may
Find pardon on my true submission.
HENRY. God pardon thee! Yet let me wonder, Harry.
The hope and expectation of thy life
Is ruined, and the soul of every man
Prophetically doth forethink thy fall.
For thou hast lost thy princely privilege
By keeping vile company. Not an eye
But is aweary of thy common sight—
Save mine, which hath desired to see thee more,
Which now doth that I would not have it do,
Make blind itself with foolish tenderness.
HAL. I shall hereafter, my most gracious lord,
Be more myself.
HENRY.   Now, by my soul,
Young Hotspur hath more title to my crown
Than thou, who claim'st it by succession.
For by no right, nor pretense like to right,
He doth fill fields with armor in the realm,
Turns head against the lion's armèd jaws,
And, being no more in debt to years than thou,
Leads agèd lords and reverend bishops on
To bloody battles and to bruising arms.
HAL. I will redeem my shame on Hotspur's head,
And, in the closing of this glorious day,
Be bold to tell you that I am your son,
When I will wear a garment all of blood
And stain my features in a bloody mask.
Today this Hotspur, this all-praisèd knight,
And your unthought-of Harry meet in arms.
For every honor sitting on his helm,
Would they were multitudes, and on my head

My shames redoubled! For the time is come
That I shall make this northern youth exchange
His glorious deeds for my indignities.
Yea, I will tear the reckoning from his heart.
This, in the name of God, I promise here;
The which if He be pleased I shall perform,
I do beseech your Majesty may salve
The long-grown wounds of my intemperance.
If not, the end of life cancels all bonds,
And I will die a hundred thousand deaths
Ere break the smallest parcel of this vow.
HENRY. A hundred thousand rebels die in this!
Command our second column.
(*Hal rides off. To the troops.*)
                             March away!
Our hopes do stand full fairly for the day!
(*He rides off. A droopier drum sound brings in Falstaff and his company
of ragamuffins — the rack of rope men, carried by Falstaff himself. Stop-
ping to catch his breath, he speaks to the audience.*)
FALSTAFF. If I be not ashamed of my soldiers, I'm a pickled
minnow. I have misused the King's draft damnably. The
householders that I impressed have bribed me to release them,
and behold the rest! One would think I'd unloaded all the
gallows on the way and drafted the dead bodies. (*Enter Hal.*)
HAL. How now, Falstaff?
FALSTAFF. Hal! How now, how now, mad wag!
HAL. Whose fellows are these that come after?
FALSTAFF. Mine, Hal, mine.
HAL. I did never see such pitiful rascals.
FALSTAFF. Tut tut, good enough to toss, food for powder,
food for powder; they'll fill a pit as well as better. Tush, man,
mortal men, mortal men.
HAL. Sirrah, make haste. Hotspur is already in the field. You
stay too long. (*He goes off.*)
FALSTAFF. Well, to the end of a fight and the beginning of a
feast
Fits a dull fighter and an eager guest.
(*He exits. Battle sounds from offstage: shouts, slapsticks, thundersheet,
etc. First single fight: Henry IV versus an anonymous Rebel —Actor 3,
wearing a full helmet. They meet, engage, and disappear fighting. During
their fight, a few rope men have been tossed on over the backdrop. They lie*

on the stage as corpses. Falstaff enters.) I would it were bedtime and all well. I am as hot as molten lead, and as heavy too. God keep lead out of me! I need no more weight than mine own bowels. I have led my ragamuffins where they are peppered. There's not one of my hundred and fifty left alive. The pay of a hundred and fifty men will purchase me many a barrel of sack. (*A Rebel — Actor 3 again — comes in and attacks him. Falstaff holds his own for a while, but when things start to go against him, he speaks aside to the audience.*) This grows too hot. 'Tis time for strategy. (*Pretending he's received a mortal wound, he howls and staggers about, then falls like a building. The Rebel exits. Enter Hotspur.*)

HOTSPUR. My sword is surfeited with common blood.
I'll fight no more till I come face to face
With that same skipping madcap Prince of Wales.
(*Hal enters. Hotspur turns to him.*)
If I mistake not, thou art Harry Monmouth.
HAL. Thou speak'st as if I would deny my name.
HOTSPUR. My name is Harry Hotspur.
HAL. Why then I see
A very valiant rebel of the name.
I am the Prince of Wales, and think not, Hotspur,
To share with me in glory any more.
HOTSPUR. I shall not, Harry, for the hour is come
To end the one of us. And would to God
Thy name in arms were now as great as mine!
HAL. I'll make it greater ere I part from thee. (*They fight. After a strenuous and even contest, Hal gives Hotspur his death wound. Hotspur falls.*)
HOTSPUR. O, Harry, thou hast robbed me of my youth. (*He dies.*)
HAL. Adieu, brave Hotspur. Fare thee well, great heart.
When that this body did contain a spirit
A kingdom for it was too small a bound,
But now two paces of the vilest earth
Is room enough. I'll cover up thy face.
(*He lays a cloak or handkerchief over Hotspur's face and starts out. Sees Falstaff.*)
What, old acquaintance? Could not all this flesh
Keep in a little life? Poor Jack, farewell!
I'll have thee disemboweled for burial.

(*He exits. Falstaff rises.*)

FALSTAFF. Disemboweled? If thou disembowel me today, I'll give you leave to salt and pepper me and eat me too tomorrow! 'Sblood, 'twas time to counterfeit, or that hot young rebel would have carved me like a kidney pie! Counterfeit? I lie, I am no counterfeit. To die is to be a counterfeit; for he is but the counterfeit of a man that hath not the life of a man. But to counterfeit dying when a man thereby liveth, is to be no counterfeit, but the true and perfect image of life indeed. The better part of valor is discretion; in the which better part I have saved my life. Zounds, I am afraid of this gunpowder Hotspur, though he be dead. How if he should counterfeit too, and rise? I'll make him sure; yea, and I'll swear I killed him. Nothing refutes me but eyes, and nobody sees me. Therefore, sirrah— (*Stabbing Hotspur's corpse.*) with a new wound in your thigh, come you along with me. (*He makes to pick up the body. Hal is heard off-stage.*)

HAL. God and your arms be praised, victorious friends.
The day is ours. The rebels all are fled.
(*Falstaff puts his foot on Hotspur as Hal comes on.*)
Art thou alive? Or is it fantasy
That plays upon my eyes? I prithee speak.
I will not trust my eyes without my ears.

FALSTAFF. There is Hotspur. If your father will do me any honor, so. If not, let him kill the next Hotspur himself. I look to be either earl or duke, I can assure you.

HAL. Why, Hotspur I killed myself, and saw thee dead.

FALSTAFF. I grant you I was down and out of breath, and so was he. But we rose both at the same time, and fought a long hour by Shrewsbury clock. If I may be believed, so. If not, let them that should reward valor bear the sin upon their own heads.

HAL. Well, Falstaff, if a lie may do thee grace
Then tell it. I will second it myself.

FALSTAFF. When I have grown great, I'll grow less. For I'll give up sack and sugar and live cleanly, as a nobleman should do. (*He toasts his resolution with an enormous hit from his wineskin.*)

HAL. (*To the troops—and the audience.*)
Rebellion in this land has lost its sway
By what we have achieved in arms today.
Now civil wounds are stopped, peace lives again.

That she may long live here, God say Amen!
(*Drum roll mounts to a climax.*)

FINIS

TEXTUAL NOTES

"Westmoreland." As often in Shakespeare, this name is pronounced two ways according to the scansion of the line that it appears in. The first time it is mentioned, the name is accented on its second syllable; the second time, on its first syllable.

"Eastcheap:" A poor district of London, noted for its rough and wild underlife.

"Sack." Spanish sherry.

"Leaping house." Another name for "brothel."

"Zounds." A swearword, short for "God's (meaning Christ's) wounds," and pronounced to rhyme with "wounds."

"Salamander." One of Falstaff's words for the drunkard Bardolph's red nose because in Shakespeare's time people thought that salamanders could live in fire.

"'Sblood." Short for "God's blood."

"Gad's Hill." A notorious stakeout for highwaymen working the road between London and Canterbury.

"Esperance." "Hope." It was part of Hotspur's family motto. It is pronounced "es-pair-*ahn*-suh."

"Drownèd." When an accent appears over the "e" of a final "ed," that syllable must be pronounced to make the line scan.

"Bacon-eaters." Consumers of expensive food; that is, the rich.

"Carbonado their shanks." Score the calves of their legs as if for broiling.

The traditional music for the song Hal sings (which is from Shakespeare's *Twelfth Night*) is as follows:

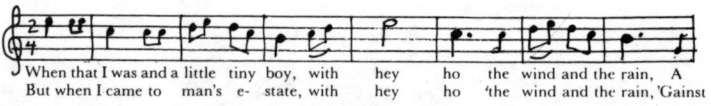

When that I was and a little tiny boy, with hey ho the wind and the rain, A
But when I came to man's e- state, with hey ho 'the wind and the rain, 'Gainst

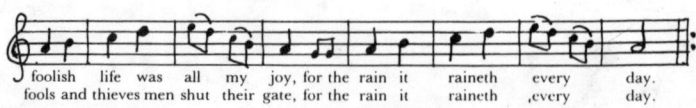

foolish life was all my joy, for the rain it raineth every day.
fools and thieves men shut their gate, for the rain it raineth ,every day.

30

"Ecce signum." Pronounced "*eh*-key *sig*-num." Latin for "This proves it."

"Tallow-catch." A pan to catch the grease from roasting meat.

"Manningtree." A town in Essex where, at annual fairs, huge oxen were stuffed and barbecued.

"Prick." To make a mark on, or actually prick a hole in, a piece of paper. Shakespeare puns on several senses of the word in a number of his plays.

"Sirrah." A word that meant "little sir," and was a sometimes disrespectful, sometimes affectionate term of address.

"Disemboweled." People of rank were often eviscerated and embalmed for burial.

The playing time for *Villainous Company* is approximately 45 minutes.

The following character and setting designations are suggested for the program:

THE CAST

(Name of Actor 1) as

AN ATTENDANT in King Henry's court

SIR JOHN FALSTAFF, a knight fallen on hard times who now resides at the Boar's Head Tavern

GILLIAMS, one of Hotspur's servants

(Name of Actor 2) as

HENRY IV, King of England

BARDOLPH, a part-time highwayman and part-time drunk

HOTSPUR, the leader of the rebellion against the King

(Name of Actor 3) as

THE EARL OF WESTMORELAND, a loyal subject of the King

HAL, the Prince of Wales, son of King Henry and the heir to his kingdom

MOLDY, SHADOW, WART, FEEBLE, BULLCALF, draft candidates for Falstaff's company of soldiers

A REBEL SOLDIER

THE SETTING

England in the Fifteenth Century

Westminster Palace
The Boar's Head Tavern
Hotspur's Quarters in the North
The Highway at Gad's Hill
A Public Street before the Boar's Head
A Field at Shrewsbury

PROPERTY LIST

Actor 1: King's crown
        King's robe
        Mug
        Lantern (possibly a fat one, to match his girth as
            FALSTAFF)
        Short-sword
        Bag of money
        Cushion (small enough to be worn on the head as a
            "crown")
        Armor breastplate or plumed helmet
        Wineskin

Actor 2: Red false nose
        Riding boots with spurs
        Rag (for shining the spurs)
        Short-sword (for the robbery)
        Broadsword (for the battle)
        Bag of money
        Cask of wine
        Two mugs
        Sheet of paper
        Pencil

Actor 3: Hat
        Wineskin
        Lantern
        Mask

Short-sword (for the robbery)
Broadsword (for the battle)
Rack of five "men" made of ropes or broomsticks
    with comical heads attached; the heads carved
    from styrofoam wig stands or other materials
Helmet
Cloak or handkerchief (to cover HOTSPUR'S face)

Offstage: Three drums, one with a "droopy" tone to it; slapsticks, thundersheets, etc., to make battle sounds

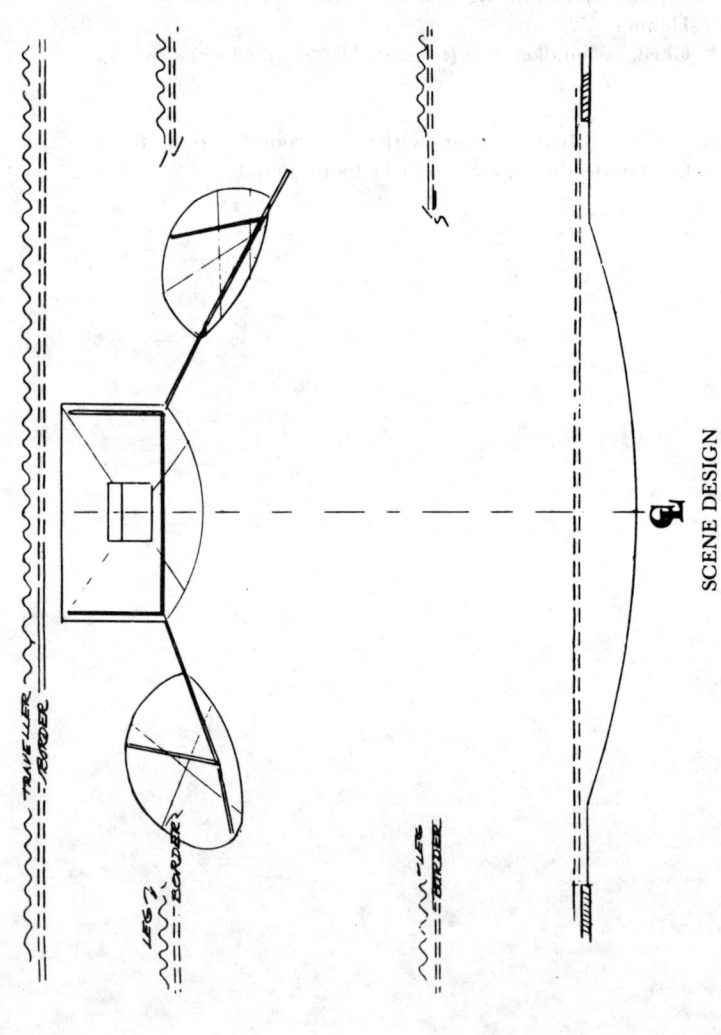

SCENE DESIGN
"VILLAINOUS COMPANY"
Designed by Laura Maurer for the Milwaukee Repertory Theater

34

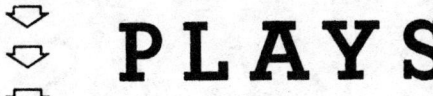

New ⇩⇩⇩ **PLAYS**

DEATHTRAP

SANTA FE SUNSHINE

THE MIDDLE AGES

TOYS IN THE ATTIC

RED ROVER, RED ROVER

THE VIETNAMIZATION OF NEW JERSEY

RIB CAGE

THE OFFERING

UNCOMMON WOMEN AND OTHERS

BRONTOSAURUS

CABIN 12

Write for information as to availability

 DRAMATISTS PLAY SERVICE, INC.
440 Park Avenue South   New York, N.Y. 10016

New

T I T L E S

BURIED CHILD

TALLEY'S FOLLY

ARTICHOKE

THE TENNIS GAME

SAY GOODNIGHT, GRACIE

OLD PHANTOMS

FAMILY BUSINESS

LATER

MASTERPIECES

THE NATURE AND PURPOSE
OF THE UNIVERSE;
DEATH COMES TO US ALL,
MARY AGNES;
'DENTITY CRISIS (One Acts)

● *Write for Information*

DRAMATISTS PLAY SERVICE, INC.

440 Park Avenue South   New York, N.Y. 10016

63

New

PLAYS

CHILDREN OF A LESSER GOD
PASSIONE
G. R. POINT
TIME AND GINGER
FATHERS AND SONS
THREE SISTERS
FULL MOON
THE ORPHANS
DUCK HUNTING
THE UBU PLAYS
TENNESSEE
THE COAL DIAMOND
WOMEN STILL WEEP
THE EXHIBITION

 DRAMATISTS PLAY SERVICE, INC.
440 Park Avenue South   New York, N. Y. 10016